A Woman, Her Influence and Impact

TWELVE DIMENSIONS THAT MAKE A WOMAN RICH

REBECCA DAIRO

Copyright © 2025 Rebecca Dairo.

All rights reserved. No part of this book may be reproduced, stored, or transmitted by any means—whether auditory, graphic, mechanical, or electronic—without written permission of both publisher and author, except in the case of brief excerpts used in critical articles and reviews. Unauthorized reproduction of any part of this work is illegal and is punishable by law.

ISBN: 979-8-89419-659-6 (sc)
ISBN: 979-8-89419-660-2 (hc)
ISBN: 979-8-89419-661-9 (e)

Because of the dynamic nature of the Internet, any web addresses or links contained in this book may have changed since publication and may no longer be valid. The views expressed in this work are solely those of the author and do not necessarily reflect the views of the publisher, and the publisher hereby disclaims any responsibility for them.

One Galleria Blvd., Suite 1900, Metairie, LA 70001
(504) 702-6708

CONTENTS

How to Use This Book iv
About the Book v
Dedication vi
Foreword vii
Reviews viii
Introduction x

Purpose #1: A Helpmeet 1
Purpose #2: A Prayer Warrior and Gatekeeper for the Holy Spirit ... 8
Purpose #3: A Manager of Resources and Time 15
Purpose #4: A Wise Woman with Diligence (Proverbs 31: 26) ... 22
Purpose #5: A Woman of Vision, Investor, Planter, Resourceful ... 27
Purpose #6: A Woman As A Manager 33
Purpose #7: A Multi-Tasker and Multiplier 39
Purpose #8: A Woman Who Seeks to Know and
                Receive from Other Kings 46
Purpose #9: A Game-Changer 54
Purpose #10: A Woman With Instructions Who Wins
                Her Enemy's Gates 58
Purpose #11: A Woman of Respect and Humility 63
Purpose #12: A Woman of Faith and Hospitality 67

Conclusion 73
References 75
About the Author 77

HOW TO USE THIS BOOK

There are 12 purposes discussed about women in this book. Ask each participant to read the discussion for each purpose #1-12, then complete the practical applications after each purpose # 1- 12 before coming to class. You can discuss this during your meeting in a small group study when you meet.

ABOUT THE BOOK

Many women face the challenge of discovering their purpose and positively impacting the world. This book explores how single and married women can achieve their goals and be key contributors to programs, homes, businesses, organizations, communities, and countries. Women who choose to marry have a responsibility to build substantial homes, support their husbands, and raise children. As they establish their households, they may discover a more fulfilling purpose beyond their initial intention of marriage. Through biblical case studies, the author highlights the significant contributions women, both single and married, have made throughout history. The book emphasizes women's unique qualities, enabling them to shine in society and become game changers. It aims to provide insights and essential attributes for women to excel and create a better world, both in their homes and communities, fulfilling God's purpose in their lives.

DEDICATION

This book is dedicated to all women who aspire to create positive changes in their homes, environments, and communities. Every woman embodies the qualities of a playmate, a warrior, and a beehive that produces honey. Ladies, it is your time to rise and become instruments of change!

I want to express my gratitude to my mother, who fought an incredible battle and emerged victorious. Her life is a testament to the idea that death can be averted through the application of God's word and the activation of the gifts, talents, and abilities that God has given us, enabling us to overcome difficulties and rise triumphantly as mighty women of God. Rather, it is our failure to utilize the gifts, talents, and abilities that God has given us that leads us to struggle during difficult times.

FOREWORD

In a society where deception has run rampant regarding what a woman truly is, Rebecca presents a genuine biblical narrative of our identity in Christ and how, through the Spirit of God, we are equipped to walk in victory. The twelve purposes of a woman, along with detailed case studies, will elevate your understanding of the word of God. It will empower you to rise above your circumstances and live the life God has called you to live. As you read this book, the Holy Spirit will ignite and awaken those hopes, dreams, and spiritual gifts!

Rebecca Dairo is a remarkable woman of God. She exemplifies what we should amplify in faith, family, church, and community. She is a woman of great humility whom God has elevated to a significant stature. This book is for everyone, whether young, middle-aged, or seasoned.

Pastor Jeanette Clark
Rivers of Living Water Church, Leesville, LA

REVIEWS

"A Woman, Her Influence and Impact" is an empowering book that celebrates the strength and contributions of women throughout history. It highlights examples of women from the Bible who played crucial roles in shaping the world we know today. The narratives are presented in an engaging and relevant manner, making it easy for readers to connect with the stories and apply the lessons to their own lives.

One of the book's strengths is its categorization of the various dimensions of a woman's life, offering insights and wisdom applicable to a wide range of situations. Whether you are a working mother, a stay-at-home wife, or a young woman just beginning your journey, "A Woman, Her Influence and Impact" has valuable lessons to share.

Overall, this book serves as an excellent resource for women seeking inspiration and empowerment. It reinforces the idea that our impact on the world is determined not by our gender but by our determination and hard work. I highly recommend it to anyone looking for guidance, support, and inspiration on their life journey.

Loretta R. Hills, 29 NOV, 2023

It makes sense to start by discussing our role as supporters of our husbands and then move on to how we function as warriors when we intercede in prayer. We manage resources and our time, among other things. The outline of your book greatly elevates women and the important roles they play in society.

Patrice Welcher, Georgia 28 NOV, 2023

As a woman of deep faith in Jesus Christ, Rebecca will help you discover your unique qualities and strengths and become a mighty woman of God. In this book, she strives to help you discover the divine gifts you possess and use them to impact your family, community, and the world.

Kathie L. Wakefield, 16 NOV 2023.

A woman, Her Influence and Impact is a valuable lesson that I learned from. I really appreciate Rebecca's approach to teaching, as she supports each topic discussed with relatable examples and Bible verses. I discovered how to rekindle love with my partner for a successful marriage, and I plan to apply all the lessons in my home. I recommend this book to my family and friends.

Adenike Fasan, Texas 15 NOV 2023.

INTRODUCTION

The concept of womanhood is an art form that expresses human creativity, producing works appreciated for their beauty. Biologically, a woman is defined as an individual with a womb who can give birth. Having a womb makes a woman unique and enables her to carry something special, enhancing her effectiveness in her endeavors. A woman is also viewed as a reflection of God's tender, loving, caring, and gentle nature, showcasing His presence in the world. Therefore, being in a woman's company is a blessing. Psalms 8:1 says, "Oh Lord, our Lord, how excellent is thy name." His name alone is excellent; therefore, anything he creates must also have excellence.

The creation story describes how God formed heaven and earth from what was once formless and empty. In the beginning, darkness covered the depths, but the Spirit of God hovered over the waters, poised for action. Only when the Spirit intervened did God begin to speak, shattering the silence. The Spirit's presence is powerful and always yields an effect. Similarly, women can bring about meaningful change, serving as conduits for God's power. Godly women who devote their lives to righteous living are endowed with a special grace that ignites a fire for change. Just as the Spirit sparked the eruption of light, both single and married women can illuminate the path to greatness in our society. Although married women are devoted to their husbands and children at home, being single or married enables them to influence people, communities, and the world around them. The emergence of light created a distinction between light and darkness, resulting in evening and morning—the dawn of a new day. This is true for all women, whether single or married, who possess the potential to foster positive change and create a new day of opportunity growth. "In the beginning, God created the heavens and the earth. Now the earth was formless and empty, darkness was over the surface of the deep, and the Spirit of God was hovering over the waters" (Genesis 1:1-2).

On the first day, something significant happened. A separation of light from darkness took place, leading to the creation of a new entity called day. This separation occurred within a vault. A woman shares similarities with this vault, as she can unveil hidden scenes and bring forth new perspectives and change. This quality may lead to challenges, but a woman is capable of addressing any difficulties that arise. If a woman, whether single or married, is aligned with her maker, she can manifest her nature to illuminate not only her problems but also the areas around her. A woman is well-equipped to solve any problem that comes up. Her skills enable her to tackle significant challenges.

A woman may be aligned with the divine nature of the Spirit of God. The Holy Spirit produces power; therefore, a woman can carry power just as the Holy Spirit does. She can reveal the supernatural nature of God, who unveils our purpose through His transcendent character and makes dreams come true. Thus, it is indeed true that a woman is compared to the Holy Spirit—an entity that carries power to you and ensures you ignite changes in the world.

What Purposes Could A Woman Have To Fulfill Her Assignment?

A woman's assignment unfolds in various phases, with different elements revealing these phases over time. Allow me to share how I was born. This true story will inspire your thoughts about how a woman transformed darkness into joy, hatred into love, scarcity into abundance, poverty into comfort, unfulfilled life into a flourishing one, and death into life through Christ. You will discover all these themes in my story birth.

Years ago, I was born to my parents, a couple with humble beginnings in a city with limited resources. One day, my mom was preparing to give birth to the baby girl now writing this book. The first challenge on the day of my delivery was how to get to the hospital. You had to be wealthy to afford a car in those days. My dad assisted my mom as she walked along the roadside. She cried for help, but there was nothing to offer assistance. My parents trekked for miles while my mother endured the pain and agony of giving birth to her first daughter. When they were halfway to the hospital, my mother could no longer lift her feet. My father, filled with compassion, knocked on another man's door and asked him to drive my mom to the hospital. This man took her there through the darkness of the night. As the nurse set eyes on my mom, she murmured the requirements before she could enter the labor room. "Requirements? Why? Isn't it accessible to everyone for free? Why now?" my dad asked.

The nurse said each woman must bring a bucket of water to deliver the baby. Every family was responsible for the water needed to clean the delivery room. At that time, water pipes were just being laid in the city, so water was not available for free. Oh my God! Both of my parents could not fetch water because the distance was too far. Therefore, my dad had to return home to get the water necessary for my delivery. A few minutes after Dad left the room, little Rebecca joyously entered the world. My mum delivered the baby, and my father returned the water he borrowed from another couple. The next phase of raising this child was another episode.

During the early phase of my life, my mom was diagnosed with asthma, a severe medical condition needing ongoing medical intervention. My family sobbed, cried, and feared my mother's early death was inevitable. Every day, I saw my mom gasping for air, looking as if she might give up the ghost. Each breath from my mom was loud and distressing, making it difficult to be around her. My dad was a tremendous, dedicated worker. Out of love, most of his paycheck went toward purchasing medications, inhalers, and other respiratory items that could help my mom survive. Life was a struggle during that time. My family struggled financially, mentally, physically, and emotionally, watching my mom's gradual decline on the bed of sickness and affliction intensified by this deadly asthma. These days were painful to remember. It's an irony of life for my family; no one could ever believe we would overcome this painful and devastating time.

My mum could have died, and my family would have thanked God for taking her away from sickness and torment. Tears dripped from my eyes every day as I went to school. Many days, I could not eat my lunch because of the fear of what her death would mean for my life and family. I was terrified every day that my mom might die before I got home from school. It was very scary and heartbreaking. I felt powerless to decide whether she lived or died, and my heart was always heavy with sorrow. Days passed, months rolled by, and years came and went, but my mom did not pass away. She was always lying down, poised to die whenever the referee of life blew the whistle of death. Hopefully, that would be her triumphant entry into eternity.

The unbelievable happened to my mom; she did not die! No, she lived and continues to live to this day. Today, she is in her seventies and enjoying a fulfilled life. What did my mom do to escape her premature death? How did she handle the situation? What motivated her to choose life instead of death? Oh, death, death, death, where was your sting? No more in my family.

My mom was delivered from death and many other challenges in life. Little Rebecca and her siblings had to hawk goods from house to house daily to put food on the table for their family. We sold food products like rice, beans, water, soft drinks, and vegetable oils. Throughout my middle and high school years, I walked about two hours to school every day for an education. There had to be a bright light ahead in the tunnel of life, or else…

During these daily struggles, my mom discovered her purpose as a woman: a revelation that changed my family's life entirely. My mom realized the power that created the unseen—that is, the nature of God in a woman who yearned to do something to save herself and her family and change her circumstances. Through the power of the Holy Ghost, my mother prayed for the strength to live and not die, to be delivered. She cried to God, "SAVE ME, SAVE ME, SAVE ME." God came to her rescue one day at a time, and today, she is a living testimony for her generation. What, then, is the purpose of every woman, and how can she make a difference for herself, her family, her circle of influence, her community, her nation, and the world?

PURPOSE #1

A Helpmeet

A woman serves as a helpmeet for her husband, complementing him in all aspects. She is not there to compete with a man but to complete him. Adam had no suitable helper; therefore, God took a rib from him and created a woman. When a woman addresses a man's needs, she invests everything into the relationship. There is an analogy with a woman's body, particularly the womb. The womb is a cavity, a space for expansion and growth. Just as her womb brings forth life, her strategies and tactics help bring ideas to fruition. As a suitable helper, her goal is to fulfill her husband's needs to create the necessary "expansion." From a literary perspective, before a woman becomes pregnant, she must receive a seed from the man. That seed is planted in her womb, and under the right conditions provided through her, it will develop into a child. Each time she receives a seed, the dynamic is unique.

A man may have a dream and hope for improvement. It takes a woman with a womb to explore the process and deliver the vision. Every woman is a unique helpmeet designed for a purpose, which is to bring abundance to her household, akin to turning a germinated seed into a baby. The nature of God within a woman allows her to reproduce and multiply anything entrusted to her. How does she influence and impact her community? She does this through strategy. Strategy generates effects that bring wealth to her home and everything she undertakes. Indeed, women are rich.

This strategy involves receiving the seed and then providing the necessary requirements, such as temperature, blood, and nourishment. This process takes nine months. This cycle repeats whenever a woman reproduces. God has bestowed this same pattern upon every woman. She can nurture any seed until it is mature enough to be born into a vision. Let me emphasize that every woman has the potential to meet the needs of her husband and family. By providing the womb to hold the seed, she can create the right conditions for the vision.

A woman relies on wisdom to nurture the seed entrusted to her and bring forth the vision of a man. The nine months needed to carry the seed requires patience, a trait every woman must possess to nurture the seed planted in her. How patient are you as a woman? What strategy do you need to nurture a seed into a vision, and how can you meet the needs of your husband, community, and nation? What impact will you make? Are you anointed and appointed to affect change in such a time as this? What actions will you take to improve everything around you?

Consider the case of Mary, who witnessed Jesus. Jesus had 12 disciples who knew about his impending death on the cross. After Jesus's resurrection, the disciples did not see him because they were too impatient to remain at the tomb. Although they received word that the master would rise on the third day, they lacked the perseverance needed to see the Lord. What a disappointment, and what foolishness on the part of the disciples! The only one who saw Jesus was a woman! Mary Magdalene was a woman who sought the Lord just like the disciples did. Her strategy was patience, that unique characteristic that allowed her to remain until she saw Jesus. She exclaimed, "Rabonni," meaning "Master." Jesus instructed her, "Do not touch me, but go and tell them that you saw me and that I am risen." Reflecting on this account, it is clear that Mary accomplished an extraordinary feat that the disciples could not. Even though they had accompanied Jesus throughout his ministry, they did not stay to see him after the resurrection. Mary's ability to be patient was a powerful strategy for witnessing Jesus after his resurrection.

Mary Magdalene helped meet the needs of the hour. She was a suitable helper who proclaimed the resurrection of Jesus at the sepulcher. At the right time, she possessed the right wisdom to fulfill God's purpose. Patience was key. She did not rush to leave; had she departed, she would have faced the same disappointment as the impatient disciples. How patient are you with your husband, children, and household? Is your patience sufficient to help bring fulfillment to your family? Do you have the wisdom to allow patience to resolve matters and fulfill God's purpose through your home, opportunities, marriage, sphere of influence, community, state, and nation?

The staying power of a woman serves as a tool to reveal what had been foretold: that Jesus would die and rise again. When a woman cultivates patience within herself, the outcome is an extraordinary experience—a unique and personalized revival that meets unexpected and profound needs. Staying and waiting are powerful tools that empower you to soar like an eagle and achieve desired results. You forfeit magnificent glory and reward when you hurry away and fail to stay.

How many homes today are broken due to the impatience of spouses? Do you frequently argue and disagree? Are you hurt and ready to leave your spouse? Why not try patience, a quality that can help you recognize the potential glory of what your home can become amidst hardships and challenges? With patience, your home will thrive rather than suffer; you and your husband will flourish instead of falter, and your relationship will expand rather than suffer and dwindle.

Helpmeet—A seed is like a woman's womb, a seed that grows and expands to become fully developed. Just like the womb nourishes the baby, delivering God's purpose requires patience and a spirit.

PRACTICAL APPLICATIONS
PURPOSE # 1: A HELPMEET

1. What does it mean to be a suitable helper in a marriage (Genesis 2 vs 18 –25)
   _____
   _____
   _____
   _____

2. In what different ways might a man need help, and how could you assist?
   a. In the family: _____
   _____
   _____
   _____

   b. As a leader, with managerial responsibilities: _____
   _____
   _____
   _____

   c. On the job/ business: _____
   _____
   _____
   _____

d. In the community or city: _____
_____
_____
_____

3. What could make you impatient?
_____
_____
_____
_____

4. How can you learn to be patient?
_____
_____
_____
_____

5. Circle one: Patient is a _____. (Read Galatians 5 vs 22-23)

   a. Gift.   b. The fruit of the spirit.

6. How does staying and waiting help you to become patient? (Isaiah 40 vs 31)
_____
_____
_____
_____

Prayer

Lord, help me to identify the purpose for living and live out to accomplish my mission here on earth. Help me to identify a strategy to lead my family into her glory, my business into a new dimension, and my community to see Jesus.

PURPOSE #2

A Prayer Warrior and Gatekeeper for the Holy Spirit

Prayer is like a gate. As discussed in my book *Building a Glorious Home: How to Construct a Fulfilling Marriage*, "I will liken prayer to your home's roof, doors, and windows. These control access to your home […] Prayer is the only savings a believer can invest toward a successful future […] Prayer gives access to the power of God and power for daily living" (Dairo, 2023). Your prayers are arrows you shoot to secure your future home. When your door is broken, or your window is left open, it signifies that your privacy and security are compromised. God allows us to guard our lives through one means—prayer. You can send prayers for your future to ensure it is secured. Life is filled with mysteries, and we have no idea what the future holds. A woman's prayer offers a unique advantage over her circumstances and whatever she aims to accomplish. A woman can travail and groan in prayer. It doesn't matter whether you are single, a single mother, or married. Travailing and groaning are special attributes that generate the force necessary to yield results.

One part of a woman is the navel. Every child you bear is nourished during pregnancy through the umbilical cord attached to the navel. Although the child is out of your womb, the umbilical cord that fed them remains significant today as a spiritual weapon. Just as a navel connects the baby to your womb for nourishment, prayer serves as the connection a woman uses to secure the future of her personal life, plans, goals, purpose, home, children, husband, community, and nation. She travails or groans. Remember, when you give birth to each child, you are prepared to pay the price to bring them forth at all costs. The hours spent in labor are not a concern for you; as long as the baby is born, you are ready to go through the process again and again. Some women undergo a caesarean section, a painful experience for managing complicated deliveries. It is about travailing, the ability to give everything it takes to bring forth the child. What will you sacrifice to bring a new purpose through you? How will you groan as a single woman, or as a single mother, or even if you are married?

The Case Study Of Hannah (Samuel 1: 15-16): Hannah, the mother of Samuel, was another example of a woman who travailed in prayer. Her rival, Peninah, constantly mocked her. She prayed until something happened, and the situation got better. As stated in the Bible, "I am a deeply troubled woman. I have not been drinking wine or beer; I was pouring out my soul to the Lord. Do not take your servant for a wicked woman; I have been praying here out of my anguish and grief."

A woman in prayer possesses a force-breaking dimension; it doesn't matter if she is single, a single mother, or married. When situations seem dark and unconducive, or when faced with opposition, prayer becomes a weapon. A woman of purpose will consistently shut her door, dedicate time for fasting, pray to the Lord, and wait for God to act. With prayer, you can unlock a closed door. Some doors might not have any keyhole; in these instances, your prayer serves as the force that must break through the door to secure access to things you have never had before. Your key will be revealed to you as a code in the spiritual realm. These codes are generated through prayer and carry a force strong enough to break the locked door. Remember, the effectual fervent prayer of a righteous person avails much. Such is the prayer of a woman. When you pray, you break the chains that bind your personal life, goals, purpose, circumstances, child-rearing, and other situations. Specific areas of life may require travailing prayer. You might face various challenges: no one in your family has ever gone to school, no one has ever married in your family, childbirth may be a difficult experience, your life may be marked by sickness and infirmity, young people may die suddenly, you may work tirelessly with nothing to show for it, you might find yourself in spiritual bondage, make little progress resulting in shame and reproach, or struggle with difficult-to-overcome addictions such as smoking or sexual issues, etc. Our schools, malls, cities, and government organizations desperately need development, expansion, and competent administrators. A woman of purpose can become an instrument that initiates prayer for change and work towards the tangible manifestation of the necessary changes. My mom relied heavily on her weapon of prayer when she was ill. Her steadfastness in worship was evident in how God transformed her health and our family, accomplishing His victory and purpose.

A WOMAN, HER INFLUENCE AND IMPACT

A woman who engages in prayer to open closed doors.

PRACTICAL APPLICATIONS
PURPOSE #2: A PRAYER WARRIOR AND GATEKEEPER FOR THE HOLY SPIRIT

1. Define prayer. Jeremiah 33 vs 3; 2 Chronicles 7 vs 14

_____

_____

_____

2. List four reasons you need to pray.(Psalm 50 vs15; Acts 16 vs 25-32; Esther 4 vs 10 -17))

a. _____

b. _____

c. _____

d. _____

3. Mention the benefits of praying (Isaiah 55 vs 6; Mark 11 vs 24)

a. _____

b. _____

c. _____

d. _____

4. What does it mean to groan in prayer? (Luke 6 vs 12; Romans 8 vs 26-27)

_____

_____

_____

_____

A WOMAN, HER INFLUENCE AND IMPACT

5. Reflect on the pain of childbirth alongside the challenges of bringing a project to life, managing a home, or facing tough times. While the pain of childbirth is profound and unique, how does it relate to other struggles we endure? What similarities and differences can we identify in these experiences?

_____
_____
_____
_____

6. Read 1 Samuel 1 vs 15 – 16

   Describe Hannah's emotions and reflect on how they relate to your own. What connections do you see, and how do her experiences enhance your understanding of your feelings?

   a. _____
   b. _____
   c. _____
   d. _____

7. What did your learn from Hannah determination to seek God's face (I Samuel 1 vs 12-16)

   c. _____
   d. _____

8. What does the prayer of a righteous do? James 5 vs 16

_____
_____

9. What does it mean to be righteous? Read Proverbs 6 vs 16-18
_____
_____

10. Mention other men that were righteous in the bible / in the circular world around you.

a. Genesis 15 vs 6_____

b. Matthew 1 vs19-21_____

c. Others _____

11. List setbacks in your family and how you go about overcoming these limitations.
_____
_____

Prayer

Take a moment to pray about what you've studied. Prayer is the key to achieving personal and communal revival in my community. Lord, help me to consistently pray for my neighborhood, community, city, state, and country for revival and for Your purpose to be fulfilled. You can write your prayer below.

PURPOSE #3

A Manager of Resources and Time

During training and deployment, soldiers receive the proper nutrition. Different strategies are involved in planning training and combat. Army commanders must double-check: Do we have enough soldiers to confront the enemy? Are there sufficient resources to feed the troops during the war? What if we cannot obtain materials for the combat zone? Do we possess what it takes to survive and win? The same principles apply during football and game training. Specialized foods help players stay fit for the game. Assistants carry the players' baseballs, helmets, and other equipment to ease the players' burden so they can focus on how to win.

A woman has a cistern, or well, which provides the right timing for action. Her cistern could represent opportunity, access to information, connections to people, the ability to remember things, wealth, beauty, money, stature, influence, education, access to children, or the ability to multitask. People are resources, and you should not overlook them. It is crucial to pay attention to four types of individuals you might encounter at any moment.

Sometimes, you need a connector who can link you to a solution for your problem. These individuals may not be wealthy or highly regarded, but they know what to do or who you need to talk to in order to resolve your issue. You must be careful not to judge people based on your emotions, preferences, or choices, but rather strive to do good to everyone. This way, you can ensure that you do not overlook or underestimate divine connectors. A divine connector may not always appear as one, but when you allow God to work through them, the blessings they produce can be remarkable. Sometimes, the advice may not seem wise, but it may be the very solution you require. During His time, Jesus spoke with a woman at the well in Samaria. This woman told Jesus that she had no husband, yet it was through her that the ministry of Jesus became known to the townspeople. In today's terms, this woman could be referred to as a single woman because Jesus revealed during their conversation that she had five husbands and the one she was with at that moment was not her husband. This woman had access to the city, which was the resource that Jesus needed. She opened the door to the resources (people) for the Lord. (John 4 vs 1- 28)

At times, influential people are essential to you. Their credibility alone can lead you to greater opportunities. They may hold the key to your growth, grant you access to an open door, offer solutions to help your family and community, or provide crucial information in a book that sets you free. Remain humble when interacting with others, as you may not fully understand the extent of God's grace in their lives. Influential individuals may take their time to respond; however, it's important to continue trusting God throughout this process *Gifted and talented people* are resources you must maintain on your team at work, business, or in the community. These people are very necessary for you to shine and bring forth your glory. Learn to be patient with people as they grow and fine-tune their talents and gifts. Be careful not to disregard people, look down on people, or relate only with your cliques. This is unhelpful to your becoming great or making a difference in your circle of influence, community, or nation.

During times of trouble and crisis, some people stick by you. They are burden bearers who help you navigate the difficult phases of life. Treasure these individuals and their commitment to you, your organization, environment, city, county, goals, and aspirations. They are very rare in our generation, but if you have anyone willing to bear a burden with you, be sure to celebrate them and keep them close. They mean more than just your blood brothers or sisters.

Beauty is a resource and a guiding principle for a woman, and she maintains herself for her man! The ability to preserve your essence for your husband and not share it with strangers is key to bringing him satisfaction. A husband can become intoxicated by her love. The same principle applies to how she uses her resources to support others at work and influence people in her community and social circle. A woman must learn to manage all her resources effectively, minimizing waste. She can be trusted with finances and can cut costs by efficiently managing available materials.

The case study of the woman with a seductive spirit (Proverbs 5: 1-23) A woman's decisions can destroy you; however, when a woman invests time in using her gifts and talents, or in nurturing her home and managing her cistern properly, she becomes a blessing. When a woman recognizes the essentials in her home, she enriches her household. Such a woman appreciates timing as a powerful tool.

Her cistern symbolizes everything she safeguards for her husband and family. For her, sex is not a means for personal gain but a reservoir to win her man. So, where does the question of who initiates sex in marriage arise? Intimacy issues are unlikely to emerge because she views her cistern as a stream that nourishes her garden. Will a woman refuse sex with her husband when there is a need? Not at all; she utilizes sex as an asset to win her man, fulfill his needs, make progress, and triumph through the power of agreement between herself and her husband. She is a treasure and a companion because of her readiness and willingness for intimacy.

Manage your time, influence, opportunities, people and resources.

PRACTICAL APPLICATIONS
PURPOSE #3: A MANAGER OF RESOURCES AND TIME

1. What are the resources you have and need to manage?

   a. _____

   _____

   b. _____

   _____

   c. _____

   _____

   d. _____

   _____

2. Why should your judgment not be based on emotions, choices or preferences? (Psalm 119 vs 11; Mark 3 vs 13-19; Luke 6 vs 12-19)

   a. _____

   _____

   b. _____

   _____

   c. _____

   _____

   d. _____

   _____

3. What does it mean to do good to everyone? (Galatians 6 vs 10; Acts 4 vs 37)

_____
_____
_____
_____
_____
_____

4. Name four people that represent any of the listed people that may be resources for you to shine either in family, business, community etc.

a. Influential people (Luke 23 vs 50-53) _____

_____
_____
_____

b. Gifted people (Genesis 41 vs 17 -31) _____

_____
_____
_____

c. Talented people (1 Samuel 16 vs 17- 23) _____

_____
_____
_____

d. Burden bearer (Luke 2 vs 22-32; Luke 2 vs 36 38) _____

_____

_____

_____

Prayer

Heavenly Father, teach me to be a faithful steward of the gifts, abilities, talents, and assignments you have entrusted to me. Please grant me the grace to honor you alone and bring value to others; may my life be a blessing in Jesus' name. Amen.

PURPOSE #4

A Wise Woman with Diligence (Proverbs 31: 26)

My family faced afflictions and storms in life, but my mom was a great pilot, guided by wisdom from the Lord. When a woman is ready to build, wisdom works through her. She is the central figure in the picture and seeks clarity about what she needs to do. Such a woman thrives on the truth of God's word and does not allow distractions. Whether faced with wind, rain, sun, thunder, calamity, famine, or sickness, or whether life is good or challenging, she gains momentum and stamina to love each member of her household or her team, despite what is happening in her life. She chooses her words wisely, aware of the consequences of unwise sayings and foolish decisions. A woman of wisdom has faithful instruction coming from her mouth (Proverbs 31:26). We live in a world where women may prefer to quit quickly on any assignment, especially when there are no results or challenges in making the desired progress. She focuses on personal development, self-awareness, self-care, dignity, integrity, and strength. Her unique self-image inspires her determination to oversee her personal affairs or her household. She remains dedicated to her assignments, goals, and purpose with faithful guidance on her tongue.

The Case Study Of Abigail (1 Samuel 25: 10-41): The story of Abigail provides insight into how a woman can build herself and give due diligence to everything around her. King David requested two things from Nabal, Abigail's husband. Nabal was required to show favor toward David's men and provide David and his servant with whatever he could find. Nabal hurled insults at David and his servants.

This insult prompted David to order the death of Nabal and his entire household. Upon learning this, Abigail devised a plan to save her family. Her wisdom protected her home from destruction. Her strategy was to maintain and preserve her household despite her husband's wicked disposition. Consider this: Abigail understood her husband's inherent nature and behaviors. She was prudent in handling her husband's hostile demeanor and recognized that no one could converse with him. Although we do not know the duration of her marriage to Nabal, Abigail coexisted with him, and he did not ruin their marriage. She fostered intimacy with the wicked man named Nabal. Her affection for him stood in stark contrast to his surly and harsh demeanor.

It is no exaggeration to say that Abigail was hardworking, intelligent, and beautiful. She was industrious and wealthy enough to manage the events in her life. Her servant remained loyal and kept her informed about current happenings. With respect, she saved her home from David's wrath. She humbled herself before David, acknowledging him as Lord. This unique approach served as a powerful tool for salvation. Just like Abigail, any woman seeking to build a business, make an impact in the community, or bring order to the chaos at home must be willing to make sacrifices and thoroughly identify strategies that safeguard their plans from various threats: enemies, winds, storms, whirlwinds, heat, rain, and so on.

A Woman Of Diligence

A WOMAN, HER INFLUENCE AND IMPACT

PRACTICAL APPLICATIONS
PURPOSE #4: A WISE WOMAN WITH DILIGENCE (PROVERBS 31 VS 26)

1. What should be the source of your wisdom? (Proverbs 2 vs 6)

_____

_____

_____

_____

2. What advantage does wisdom give you? (Proverbs 1 vs 1-4; Proverbs 11 vs 14; 2 Chronicles 1 vs 10)

a. _____

_____

b. _____

_____

c. _____

_____

d. _____

_____

3. Mention sacrifices you need to make to end chaos for each listed area:

a. home: _____, _____, _____

_____

b. business: _____, _____, _____
_____

c. city: _____, _____, _____
_____

d. country: _____, _____, _____
_____

e. Others_____: _____, _____, _____
_____

4. List 4 events that may represent storms of life that requires wisdom to come over.

a. _____
_____

b. _____
_____

c. _____
_____

d. _____
_____

Prayer

Oh Lord, I proclaim your word in Proverbs 22:29 into my life. I decree and declare that I will excel in my work, that I will stand before kings and not before unknown men. I can do all things through Christ who strengthens me and will be celebrated for excellence. Amen.

PURPOSE #5

A Woman of Vision, Investor, Planter, Resourceful

(Proverbs 31: 16-18)

A woman's vision leads to her first assignment: answering the question of her purpose within her immediate environment. This environment may include her family, her workplace, and more. Her goal could be to support and raise responsible, obedient children—physically, emotionally, and financially. This woman remains mindful of her own behavior and that of her children in society. Whether she is single or married, her aim is to raise children who contribute positively to society, irrespective of gender. Investing her time means paying close attention to her children at home, utilizing various resources and skills to nurture their nature in a manner that benefits humanity. Everything she possesses—her experience, passion, education, and submission to her husband or any authority—is essential. Her willingness to submit to authority reflects her humility, a truly invaluable quality. Humility not only helps her gain favor from her husband and superiors but also attracts the attention of God and His angels, guiding her and her household in all endeavors. This woman is accountable to God and open to allowing other leaders to direct her path toward fulfillment.

Vision is the framework that allows one to see the current state of a situation, recognize its shortcomings or inefficacies, and cultivate the desire to identify new ideas or strategies that can address existing problems while communicating potential possibilities that inspire change. These changes may motivate other family members, individuals, or community members to shift their perspectives. When a woman is a visionary, she actively works to solve problems, often putting in long hours and going the extra mile to achieve her goals. Although challenges may threaten her plans, she is equipped with strength and dignity to endure even the toughest times.

The storm of sickness that swept through my family was fierce, but it couldn't dismantle my parents' relationship. As I mentioned earlier, we sold goods from house to house; these efforts were my mom's clever strategy to sustain our family during hardship. Her vision centered on how to keep the family afloat and survive challenging times. This principle applies to any woman who perceives the light at the end of the tunnel. She must dedicate time to her family's vision for it to prosper. She wholeheartedly supports her husband to ensure that all family needs are met. Today, women can earn income and invest in their futures through various avenues. These investments may involve purchasing cryptocurrencies, engaging in foreign exchange, earning through trades, pursuing education, working in government positions, sewing, painting, technological advancements, military careers, small businesses, healthcare, social work, and entrepreneurship etc.

The case study of the woman in Proverbs 31: Proverbs 31 describes a woman, yet her name remains unmentioned. Thus, this woman could represent anyone who embodies the character portrayed. She was exceptional, as her righteousness surpassed that of others. This woman had a vision; she was likened to a merchant ship, with her aspirations extending far beyond her immediate surroundings. She looked well beyond herself and her current situation. Within her was a vision born from the perception of a distant place. This woman was not idle; her desire for her family was clear, and she actively pursued it. She was strong, earned an income, and provided nourishment for her family. She worked diligently, evaluated a field, purchased it, and then invested her earnings by planting a vineyard. At night, she remained awake, her light never extinguishing. Her husband gained respect not for his actions, but for hers. Her deeds elevated him among the elders of the land, bestowing upon him honor solely due to her character and determination. It is evident that a woman with vision does not partake in the sustenance of an idle person.

A Woman With A Vision

PRACTICAL APPLICATIONS
PURPOSE #5: A WOMAN OF VISION, INVESTOR, PLANTER, RESOURCEFUL

1. What is your vision?

a. home: _____

_____

b. workplace: _____

_____

c. Community: _____

_____

d. Others: _____

_____

2. Describe five different qualities you have and how you can use these qualities to realize your vision?

a. _____

_____

b. _____

_____

c. _____

_____

d. _____
_____

e. _____
_____

3. Do you have a vision? What problems do you like to solve?

a. Family _____
_____

b. Organization/ work _____
_____

c. Community _____
_____

4. How can you invest your time and avoid becoming idle? (Luke 4 vs 16; 1 Kings 19 vs 19-21)

_____
_____
_____
_____
_____

Prayer

Lord, I ask for wisdom and knowledge to be a resourceful woman, kindhearted and sensitive to the needs of my immediate family and others, so that I may bless them with the gifts, talents, influence, grace, and opportunities you have given me, all to the glory and honor of your name.

PURPOSE #6

A Woman As A Manager

A woman with a purpose holds a managerial assignment. You might not have the title of a manager, but your role requires you to unify the various people and tasks associated with you. Being a manager is not merely a title, but a position that demands wisdom in overseeing all aspects of your life. A woman must be a good steward of her time, resources, and assets, as well as a manager of people, including children, family members, and her community. Initially, your responsibility may be just to care for yourself. Then, you can tend to your immediate family and gradually take on more responsibilities at work, in your church, community, and business. If a woman has a purpose for her business, workplace, community, county, and nation, she must be able to answer specific questions that help guide her assignment and fulfill her roles. According to a YouTube presentation by the Apostle Joshua Selman in a speech titled "How to build formidable systems and structures in your life," fulfilling your roles requires you to have a system in place.

Selman discussed six questions that anybody can use to build a formidable system and structure. These questions were posed to anyone who plans for success. They are presented here tailored specifically towards the mission and assignment of a woman:

1. Why do you exist as a woman, and what can you offer to your home, community, and organization?
2. Who will benefit from my assignments as an individual, wife and an employee, and how can I invest my time to assist them?
3. What resources, skills, and relationships do you have to complete your assignments?
4. How do you plan to distribute the tasks at on your business, home, at your job, in the community, or your circle of influence?
5. What are the priorities and emphasis for your home, job, business, city, place of work, country now? Do you need to build up the people first, that is, build a relationship with your husband and children? Do you need to build your rapport with your organization, employees and then create unique products and services that will make programs successful?
6. What limitations, pitfalls, and distractions must be avoided? What prideful attitudes and inappropriate relationships may not be helpful to achieving your goals?

The managerial role of a woman involves distributing tasks to her family members based on their age or abilities. In an organization, a purposeful woman recognizes the talents of individuals and understands what they are skilled at. She identifies the strengths and capabilities of her team members and the areas where they can excel. Her strength lies in maximizing her potential and training others to achieve mastery in their work. This woman does not let jealousy, insecurity, or a sense of superiority control her. With a calm demeanor, she aims to achieve the best outcomes given the opportunities and the people she collaborates with. She reflects on uncovering the reasons behind every appointment she receives or every disappointment she experiences.

The case study of Deborah: Deborah was a prophetess and a leader of the Israelites. Little is known about her husband, Lapidoth. The Bible does not describe his job, position, influence, wealth, education, or accomplishments. It seems that Deborah was more extroverted and outgoing than her husband. She served as a judge for Israel, where the Israelites came to her for dispute resolution. To function as a judge, Deborah had to be knowledgeable about the law, family matters, land, health, wealth, taxes, and various aspects of life. She was a proficient manager of time and resources, at the forefront of affairs, and a dynamic leader who judged both the rich and the poor, the educated and the uneducated, and skilled and unskilled men and women of Israel. As a manager, she did not let intimidation, feelings of inferiority, or perceptions of superiority influence her decision-making. Sisera commanded an army with nine hundred chariots and treated Israel harshly for twenty years. Deborah recognized what Israel needed to do. She called for Barak, the commander of Israel, and instructed him to lead the nation into battle against Sisera at Mount Tabor. Deborah's managerial ability was clear, as she understood the mind of God and knew that Israel's deliverance was imminent. As a leader, a woman in authority must comprehend God's intentions to make decisions during difficult times. Barak clearly recognized the kind of leader Deborah was. He would not go to war without her by his side. What an honor!

A woman's transparency at home, work, and in business will inspire others to collaborate with her. Her humble heart and spirit will make a man want her to be involved in government affairs and leadership.

The only condition for Barak to go to war was that Deborah would accompany him. This illustrates the trust and confidence Barak had in Deborah. As a manager, a woman must view submission as a tool that helps her win a man's heart. This may lead to greater responsibility and the ability to accomplish more tasks. Israel's resources were far less than Sisera's, yet Deborah understood that the Lord's way is not reliant on the number of people available, but rather that God can grant victory even with limited resources. As a woman submits to God, discernment becomes a vital aspect of her character. Discernment is the ability to understand the reasons behind an action. If she can discern accurately, she gains insight into how to address issues wisely and succeed in all her endeavors. If there is to be a change in our nation, the presence of a woman who fears God and seeks transformation will make a significant difference at any level in government, business, education, healthcare, the military, churches, and civil society. Deborah understood her purpose, her mission to the nation of Israel, and her relationship with Barak, which allowed her to influence him in helping Israel triumph over the enemy that had oppressed the nation for over twenty years. Finally, with God's assistance, the enemy was defeated. Barak and Deborah sang a song of victory together. The song read,

> "Villagers in Israel would not fight; they held back
> until I, Deborah, arose, until I arose, a mother in Israel"
> (Judges 5:7).

PRACTICAL APPLICATIONS
PURPOSE #6: A WOMAN AS A MANAGER

1. Name the possible talents of people on your team

   a. _____

   b. _____

   c. _____

   d. _____

   e. _____

2. What action should you explore to avoid each of the following:

   a. Jealousy _____

   b. Insecurity _____

   c. Offense _____

   d. Sense of Superiority _____

3. Why do you exist as a woman, and what can you offer to your home, community, and organization?
   _____

4. Who will benefit from my assignments as an individual, wife, and employee, and how can I invest my time to assist them?
   _____

5. What resources, skills, and relationships do you have to complete your assignments?
   _____

6. How do you plan to distribute the tasks at on your business, home, at your job, in the community, or your circle of influence?
   _____

7. What are the priorities and emphasis for your home, job, business, city, place of work, and country now? Do you need to build up the people first, that is, build a relationship with your husband and children?
   _____

8. What rapport do you need to build with your organization and employees?
   _____

9. What unique products and services do you need to create that will make programs successful?
   _____

10. What limitations, pitfalls, and distractions must be avoided? What prideful attitudes and inappropriate relationships may not be helpful to achieving your goals?
    _____

Prayer

Take a moment to reflect on what you learned from this lesson. Identify the specific areas where you are struggling. Bring your challenges before the Lord in prayer, asking for guidance and clarity to help you overcome them.

PURPOSE #7

A Multi-Tasker and Multiplier

It is well known that women are capable of multitasking. This unique ability allows them to juggle various assignments and projects. However, caution is necessary when multitasking, as it can lead to working on too many tasks without achieving specific outcomes. This may result in wasted time and hinder your pursuit of success. Question Number 5 above asks, "What are the priorities and areas of focus for your home, job, business, city, workplace, and country at this time?" Answering this question can help you address the challenges associated with multitasking. It is important to recognize the immediate needs and determine what actions must be taken. This clarity aids in prioritizing the most critical tasks above less urgent ones. You need to be precise regarding your assignments, or you risk spending time on tasks that do not contribute to your business goals. Does your business require a consultant to support your growth and expansion? Should you train individuals to acquire special skills and certifications necessary for success in their roles? If the assignments pertain to home, you may need to assess which areas require growth for family members. Do they need to learn about prayer, communication, cooking, understanding each other, or enhancing their emotional intelligence? Do your husband and children need to improve their relationships with one another and society? Is there a need to educate your family about savings and financial investment? Should children be taught how to manage chores?

What areas require improvement if you want to implement changes at work? Do you need enhancements in production or human resources? Is there a need to improve the integration of technology, including software and hardware necessary for production? Does your organization require new training to enhance human resources efficiency and reduce waste? Do you need to identify key individuals within the organization who can facilitate improvement in each department and ensure overall growth? Should you consider shifting personnel at lateral or cross-lateral levels to achieve your desired outcomes? Your ambitions for your circle of influence involve identifying other female leaders possessing skills necessary for driving change within an organization.

You should devise a formula to learn about each product or service and optimize its productivity. Selman defined a system as an organized approach or "a set of principles or procedures according to which something is done." A system represents an executed strategy, or a collection of elements organized for a common purpose. To better understand what a system and structure entail, let's explore two examples. The first example is the operation of a television. The manufacturer designs the television so that any purchaser can easily follow the manual and operate it. Regardless of where you place the TV, if you adhere to the manufacturer's instructions, it will function effectively. This is due to the manufacturer having established a system to assist end users in operating the TV. The second example is the human body. The body comprises various components, each with its specific functions. Medical schools equip doctors with the instructions necessary to comprehend how the body operates and which medications treat particular diseases. Doctors might be trained in diverse states and institutions, but they all undergo similar specialized training that guides their medical practice. Two doctors from different states can consult about a patient and communicate with professionalism, irrespective of their different training backgrounds. No matter the country, if a doctor is trained according to the medical practice system, they will understand what the other practitioner is conveying. Similarly, you can establish a system within your home, organization, community, or nation. You will be amazed at how effectively you can achieve results and ensure the smooth operation of the organization.

The case study of Mary and Martha (Luke 10: 38-41): Martha had so much energy for work and wanted to please Jesus. She thought she would be noticed for doing many things and receive praise from Him. Her hope was shattered when Jesus rebuked her for the distractions her preparations caused. Martha asked Jesus to tell Mary to help her. What a disappointment that she did not even understand the Master's intent and what He desired. Mary was focused, and her approach was systematic. She understood that the most important thing was to be seated at the Lord's feet to learn. If you consistently implement this approach, it will yield the right results time and again. Do not rush to become a manager if you have not learned enough to produce results. In fact, if you think you know everything, it is wise to sit back and let others handle tasks that you are familiar with. You will be amazed at the things you didn't know and still need to learn. This is wisdom for anyone looking to see results in business or home life.

"Martha, Martha," the Lord answered,
"you are worried and upset about many things,
but only one thing is needed. Mary has chosen what
is better, and it will not be taken away from her"
(Luke 10:41).

A Woman Is a Multitasker

PRACTICAL APPLICATIONS
PURPOSE # 7: A MULTITASKER AND MULTIPLIER

1. Discuss ways to foster growth for your family members on the list below:

i. Communication: _____

ii. Prayer Life: _____

iii. Studying the bible: _____

iii. A New Skill _____

iv. Emotional Intelligence: _____

v. Financial knowledge/discipline: _____

vi. Community service: _____

vii. Others _____

2. Discuss other areas where your family requires growth.

a. Discuss how you plan to implement values such as integrity, honesty, faithfulness, commitment, ethics, morality, and conscience to help your children and their education.

_____

b. Discuss certain things you should restrict to help children build their values.

_____

c. What other activities can children be engaged in to limit screen time and ensure dedication to academic and personal growth?

_____

d. What habits and behaviors are most important to you in your home?
___

3. Business/ community
i. What consultation do you require to help your expansion?
___

ii. Does your organization require new training to enhance the efficiency of the people?
___

iii. Do you need to identify key individuals within the organization who can facilitate improvement in each department and ensure overall growth?
___

iv. Should you consider shifting personnel at lateral or cross-lateral levels to achieve your desired outcomes?
___

v. What system represents an executed strategy that helps improve the production of products and services in your business and organization?
___

vi. Discuss specific actions, operations, or systems within your home, organization, or community. Have you identified what may improve efficiency and ensure the smooth operation of the organization, leading to results and expansion?
___

vii. What areas do you need to improve yourself that may promote results in your family life, business, and community?

Prayer

What areas in our lives—family, business—need transformation? A change in mindset? Write them down and ask God to intervene and turn them around for good. Lord, help my unbelief; give me grace to trust in Your word and not in my understanding. Things may not seem to be where I want them to be, but I will trust in You, for I know that all things work together for good for those who love You and are called according to Your purpose.

PURPOSE #8

A Woman Who Seeks to Know and Receive from Other Kings

Nobody likes change, or rather, implementing change can be very challenging. It may provoke pushback, or others might need to witness the positive effects that changes can bring. Realizing change comes at a cost. You must be selfless, willing to make sacrifices, and focused on your goal if there is to be any improvement in your business, at home, or at any organizational level. Implementing systems and structure is a valuable means of achieving the necessary change. The word "structure" originates from the Latin word "structura," meaning to build or fit together or how the parts of a system are arranged (Cambridge Dictionary, 2023). Structure informs you of how things are made. With structure, you can position a component in a specific area and have it fit perfectly because it complies with the established system. A lack of structure anywhere breeds chaos and makes progress unsustainable. Outcomes become unpredictable when structure is absent. Therefore, for a woman to see results in her business, at home, and in any other endeavor she invests her time in, she must create a formula or approach that ensures efficiency among the various components involved. A single process and standard are essential because you desire great results. You will achieve few or no results whenever there is a double standard. Such homes and organizations will experience chaos. Favoritism based on color, gender, preferences, and biases will undermine any organization or system community.

You need to be cautious about how your emotions may influence your actions. Women are known for being very emotional, a trait that defines them. However, acting solely on your feelings can lead to ruin or disaster in your business, home, organization, or any other areas where you seek growth. Chapter eight of my book, Building a Glorious Home, emphasizes the importance of guarding your emotions much like you would install a fence around your property. Allow the Word of God to guide your choices and actions.

The result drives your motives and actions. To sustain results and continue achieving outcomes, you must minimize biases based on opinions about age, sex, gender, race, nationality, and personal views. Your approach needs to reproduce results in different places and among various people, with or without your presence. Therefore, the plan should provide guidance for others, including different regions and nations. The outcome will be consistent and will yield outstanding results. Jesus demonstrated to the early church how they should live. He taught the disciples how to fast and pray for specific effects to manifest in their lives in ministry.

Having two important things in place makes it easy for you to create positive change:

1. Create a value system or code of conduct for every event, service, or product (Selman, 2022). What are your values for the children and their education? Are there certain things that you should restrict to help children build their values? Do you plan to restrict screen time to ensure dedication to academic and personal growth? What habits do you encourage your husband, children, and anyone to demonstrate in the home? What are your values for employees at work? Do they have to complete certain training that helps promote appropriate customer service at any level in the organization? What is the code of conduct for arrival at and departure from work? Do they need to punch in and out? Are employees recorded on security cameras in case there is any misconduct?

2. Create an operational guide that describes how things are done based on your convictions and priorities (Selman, 2022). For example, what is the procedure for promotion in the organization? How is an employee recruited? In a home setting, what are the kids' limits for screen time? What are the discipline procedures for the children? What are offenses for which your children need redirection? What may lead to dismissing an employee from duty? Operational guides provide a system that allows you to be fair and achieve greater results in the home and any organization.

The Case Study Of The Queen Of Sheba (1 Kings 10: 1-13): Queen Sheba heard of King Solomon's wisdom. When she visited him, she was overwhelmed by the food on his table, the robes of his attendants, the burnt offerings he sacrificed at the Lord's temple, and the seating of his officials and cupbearers. Though she was royalty, she did not sit down merely to mock Solomon. She was a dynamic woman who sought to witness for herself what she had been told. She pursued knowledge from another king. She acknowledged the great wisdom of Solomon, the happiness of his officials in his palace, and his magnificent wealth. She brought more spices to King Solomon from her riches than anyone else had before. She extended her hand to the king. Despite her wealth, King Solomon granted the Queen of Sheba all she desired from the royal bounty. She received gifts that enabled her to build a better kingdom. A wise queen, indeed! When a woman recognizes the splendor and remarkable achievements of another royal, she earns favor that can enhance her knowledge and the capabilities of her kingdom.

Are you open enough to receive guidance, lessons, wisdom, training, studies, and gifts from others, or does your pride prevent you from accepting help and assistance? Do you believe you have everything sorted out, don't need anyone's assistance, and feel superior to others? Sometimes, you must allow others to handle certain tasks you're capable of, or even pay for those services. Doing so gives you time to pray, spend time with or visit your children, and cherish moments with your husband or loved ones. If you find that your efforts yield little to no results, it may be wise to let others assist you, or learn from professionals in that field. The willingness to learn and accept help from others is indeed a strength. The world may encourage you to outshine others through destruction, but true success does not come from outperforming those around you. When we extend recognition to others and appreciate their greatness, they are more likely to support us and empower us to achieve greatness ourselves. You might even become even more exceptional. A woman who seeks knowledge understands how the great can assist her "King Solomon gave the queen of Sheba all she desired and asked for, besides what he had given her out of his royal bounty" (1 Kings 10:13).

PRACTICAL APPLICATIONS
PURPOSE #8: A WOMAN WHO SEEKS TO KNOW AND RECEIVE FROM OTHER KINGS

1. Describe a significant change that will help you maintain focus on your goal if there is to be any improvement in your business, at home, or in any organization or community setting.

   _____
   _____

2. Create a formula or approach that ensures efficiency among the various components involved in your home, business, and community.

   _____
   _____

3. What processes and standards are essential to promote results?

   _____
   _____

4. Identify areas that demonstrate double standards in your home and organization. How will you address double standards in the future?

   _____
   _____

5. Discuss ways to minimize or avoid biases related to age, sex, gender, race, nationality, and personal beliefs.

_____
_____

6. Discuss the day(s) and time you fast and pray for specific effects to manifest in your lives, business, and ministry. (Daniel 10 vs 2)

_____
_____

7. Explore how the Word of God can illuminate your decisions and shape your emotions. How can its wisdom guide your choices and influence your feelings in everyday life?

_____
_____

8. What are the screen time boundaries for kids when it comes to a home environment?

_____
_____

9. Share some exciting reward ideas and effective discipline strategies for guiding children(Proverbs 22 vs 6; Ephesians 6 vs 4)

_____
_____

10. What are some behaviors and moments when your children might need a gentle nudge in the right direction? (Proverbs 22 vs 15)

_____

_____

11. Describe training that can be outsourced to enhance employees' lives and improve job performance. This training may include goal setting, leadership development, life coaching, parenting skills, safety awareness, family dynamics, relationship management, technology utilization, data analysis, and emotional intelligence self-regulation.

_____

_____

12. Discover individuals who have achieved outstanding success in their homes and businesses or made a significant impact in their communities. What unique strategies or qualities contributed to their excellence that you can learn from? (1 Kings 3 vs 9-15; Genesis 13 vs 2; Galatians 3 vs 6-9)

_____

_____

Prayer

Consider the decisions you need to make regarding the changes God has placed in your heart for your family, your life, your business, your marriage, and your ministry or organization. Lord, please open the eyes of my heart; I want to see you. Show me your way and your will. Teach me to understand the times and what actions I need to take.

PURPOSE #9

A Game-Changer

Fearless women comprehend the mysteries of life and can endure various circumstances and opposition. The chameleon's survival strategy is to blend in with the colors of her environment. With this approach, the chameleon need not worry about threats. These threats may exist, but she crafts a plan to outsmart them. Such is the method of an overcomer; any woman who intends to rise above the current economic situation and achieve success must be a game-changer. A game-changer alters the rules of her environment. Anything intended for evil can transform into good; anything deemed impossible can become possible because there are ways to implement change.

Pressure from lack of results or adversaries may create tension, struggle for power, shame, and dishonor, among other things. However, when a woman identifies a divine strategy, it can change the sequence of events, defeat the enemy, silence opposition, subdue dissenters, and redeem her through her sacrifices for others.

The Case Study Of Esther: Esther was a woman like you and me. She achieved extraordinary feats for her generation. She prevented the destruction of her nation by a single man. She recognized the right time to implement a strategy. When a woman has a vision, her goal extends beyond herself. Her imagination saves her, her program, her household, her friends, her people, her children, her youth, her community, her state, and her nation. Esther's vision was systematic. She carefully influenced the enemy's affairs and saved her province. She stopped the destruction of the Jews and reclaimed the entire nation. What a victory, indeed!

Such was the approach that brought redemption to the world. Jesus came with a mission to seek and save the lost. This mission of redemption was met with opposition from the elders, the leaders of synagogues, Pharisees, and Sadducees. The Lord walked through the midst of this opposition and submitted to the cross. Christ was nailed to the cross and died. He rose again on the third day. What the enemy intended became the measure of our victory through death and sacrifice on the cross. He died and rose again. He fought against four different powers: sin, death, the grave, and Hades, and was resurrected. This led to our redemption and eternal life through Christ Jesus "Therefore, there is now no more condemnation for those that are in Christ Jesus **because, through Christ Jesus, the law of the Spirit who gives life has set you free from the law of sin and death**" (Romans 8:1).

My mom had to battle through illness. She fought hard, but all the glory belongs to God. Now, her baby (Rebecca) can write this book today to bless others, and you can witness the power of the Savior at work through Jesus Christ.

PRACTICAL APPLICATIONS
PURPOSE # 9: A GAME CHANGER

1. What areas need changes in your personal life, workplace, business, and community?
   _____
   _____
   _____
   _____

2. What strategy may be needed to improve performance in your home, programs, events, behaviors, habits etc.
   _____
   _____
   _____
   _____

3. Can you imagine a strategy that will overthrow your spiritual enemy's and adversary's plans for your progress?
   _____
   _____
   _____
   _____

4. If you have to fight a good fight, what will the fight be? What result will you expect from the fight (Read 1 Timothy 6 vs 12; 1 Timothy 1 vs 18)

_____
_____
_____
_____

5. What do you understand by "keeping the faith"? Read 2 Timothy 4 vs 7)

_____
_____
_____
_____

Prayer

Oh God, my Lord, according to your word I put on the whole armor of God because I know that my battle is against the wiles of the devil, for I wrestle not against flesh and blood, but against the rulers of the darkness of this age, against spiritual hosts of wickedness in the heavenly places.

PURPOSE #10

A Woman With Instructions Who Wins Her Enemy's Gates

A woman has the power within her. As a woman, you can become a treasure waiting to be discovered because of what you carry. When she welcomes the Holy Spirit, the ordinary woman transforms into a better version of herself, worthy of admiration. You will see her operating at a higher level, accomplishing new and more significant things than one can imagine. The Word of God renews her strength, and the words she speaks hold a power that brings about change and expansion. With the Word of God, she can command the day to unfold with glory. A woman's faith can summon the supernatural, and her spoken commands can shift the supernatural realm. This tool reveals the many dimensions of God at work in a situation. This woman does not succeed with her emotions because she draws from a strength beyond her humanity. Her victories are strategic and come through the Word of God. She declares life over her business, circumstances, home, job, ministry, family, nation, and community, breaking cycles of pain and negative experiences. She does this by nurturing a vision that will give rise to improvement, change conditions, enhance systems, eliminate lack and poverty, enlighten the people, rectify past and present mistakes, and provide direction for a glorious future. Her innovations and interventions bring light to a dark world, hope for the hopeless, prosperity for those in need, and revival to a city nation.

The Case Study Of Esther (Esther 4 vs 1-17): Esther asked the Jews in Susa to fast and pray for her for three days without eating or drinking. She and her attendants did the same. This spiritual practice gave her the strength to fulfill her mission before approaching the king. Her guidance offered insights that would aid her in accomplishing her task and overcoming her adversary. The confidence she felt in confronting the king stemmed from the power she generated through the spirit. She viewed the battle from a spiritual perspective rather than a physical one. After this, Mordecai departed from Esther and followed her instructions. A woman with a purpose is fearless and can confront any situation, regardless of the consequences that may arise.

A Woman Of Prayer and Fasting

PRACTICAL APPLICATIONS
PURPOSE # 10: A WOMAN WITH INSTRUCTIONS WHO WINS HER ENEMY'S GATES

1. Identify instances and cycles of pain in the following areas:

a. Family: _____

_____

b. Personal life: _____

_____

c. Business: _____

_____

d. Ministry: _____

_____

e. Community: _____

_____

2. How will you overcome the pain listed above:

a. Improves performance: _____

_____

b. Eliminates lack: _____

_____

c. Change inappropriate conditions: _____

_____

d. Rectify past and present mistakes: _____
_____

e. Others: _____
_____

3. Pause and think of innovations that can bring light and illumination for improvements in your home, circle of influence, workplace, business, etc.

_____
_____
_____
_____
_____

4. How do you plan to incorporate prayer and fasting time into your home, personal life, business endeavors, ministry, etc.?

_____
_____
_____
_____
_____

5. Discuss the power of prayer and fasting and the results you got when you engaged these tools in your daily activities (Esther 4 vs 1-17; Daniel 6 vs 10-11; Daniel 6 vs 21-23).

_____
_____
_____
_____
_____

Prayer

Take a moment to reflect on the lessons you gained from this study. Lord, teach me how to pray; show me how to fast and pray. I seek to understand the profound secrets of prayer, so that I may pray with fervor and effectiveness. Amen.

PURPOSE #11

A Woman of Respect and Humility

When a woman shows respect, she can win her husband's heart. Our generation often lacks respect for one another in marriage, relationships, society, and community. A woman's respect reflects her attitude toward her husband and others. When a woman wears respect like a robe, it becomes evident. Respect is a tool that secures access, favor, and acceptance. Respect helps you see yourself as lower than your true worth; you can elevate others and hold them in high regard. Many people believe respect comes from academic achievements, position, fame, wealth, job status, or possessions. While all these factors can earn respect, your true worth doesn't stem from them, as they can be fleeting. Someone might be poor yet still fail to respect others. Pride is a matter of the heart and can manifest in anyone, regardless of their level, status, or wealth etc.

The Case Study Of Bathsheba And Solomon's Coronation: Bathsheba was a woman who altered her enemies' plans to secure the future of the Jews. Shortly after she learned that Adonijah had taken over the kingdom without King David's knowledge, she met with the king to discuss it. Her approach was respectful, as Bathsheba bowed before the king, prostrating herself to him before making any requests. (1 Kings 1: 16). Although she knew God planned for Solomon to become king, her approach was subtle. How do you respect your husband or another man? You speak of the man in high reference. You praise the man for who he is and hold him in high regard. A man does not need love, but when you respect him, you can win his trust and have a place in his heart. This principle applies to all men and women.

PRACTICAL APPLICATIONS
PURPOSE # 11: A WOMAN OF RESPECT AND HUMILITY

1. What do you understand about respecting others? (1 Kings 1 vs 16; Ephesians 5 vs 21)

   _____
   _____

2. How do you respect other people? (James 4 vs 6-7)

   _____
   _____

3. Why should you respect other people? (Ephesians 5 vs 21; I Peter 3 vs 1 &7)

   _____
   _____

4. Is there a correlation between respect and humility?

   _____
   _____

5. How do you demonstrate pride from your heart? (Proverbs 18 vs 12)

   _____
   _____

6. Does poverty or wealth indicate humility?

_____
_____

7. Explain the sentence "pride goes before destruction"? (Proverbs 16 vs 18)

_____
_____

8. How can you avoid pride in your heart? (Colossians 3 vs 17).

_____
_____

9. What are the rewards God gives a humble man? (James 4 v 6 and 10)

_____
_____

Prayer

Lord, I profess your word from the book of Ephesians 4:2 into my life. Help me to be completely humble and gentle; help me to be patient, bearing with one another in love. Amen.

PURPOSE #12

A Woman of Faith and Hospitality

Before a house is built, a blueprint translates the idea into the physical structure. This principle applies to anything requiring a tangible outcome. It's important to recognize that faith is necessary to produce results for your home and organization. You must first use faith to create something in the spiritual realm before it can manifest physically. So, what is faith? Faith involves taking a risk. It requires you to build twice. First, in the spiritual realm, you need a positive outlook toward achieving a specific result. Faith compels you to trust God, and you do this through prayer. Your spiritual senses will awaken as you dedicate time to prayer. Once activated, these senses will help you receive insights from the scriptures that will guide your path. As you patiently wait in faith and depend on God, your mind generates ideas and creativity that direct your actions. Second, in the physical realm, you combine these ideas to reach your desired outcome. A woman's faith is powerful because it can create a strategy that yields excellent results. Over time, her methods become clear and can, after being tested and proven effective, be standardized into a blueprint for others to follow and replicate due to their consistent outcomes.

As your faith drives you to pray, you will turn your attention to people and circumstances. Prayer transcends mere words; it serves as a tool for enlightenment. Engaging in prayer transforms you into a new person when you confront various situations. Rather than merely seeing challenges, failures, or shortages, you will cultivate compassion and mercy to address these shortcomings. Prayer provides you with strategic insights for dealing with your situation. You will refuse to settle for mediocrity, seeking instead the knowledge that elevates you. You will pray until you witness God's extraordinary actions in your projects, assignments, organizations, businesses, families, communities, and nation. Your prayer becomes a weapon that subdues the forces of darkness and a conduit through which God is glorified in the body.

Through prayer, you will make declarations, spiritual laws, and requests to God to receive His promises. When you prioritize prayer in your home, you will discover and harness extraordinary things throughout your life. Prayer empowers you to combat threats to your home's prosperity and triumph in your personal and organizational endeavors. My mom is a woman of prayer; her life centers around the word of God. She wished to see God glorified in her life or death. Through prayer, she overcame the pains of death and became victorious.

As people are drawn to you, you become welcoming to them. Hospitality involves accepting and hosting guests, visitors, or strangers in your environment. When you practice hospitality, you meet and support others' needs, whether emotional, physical, educational, social, or mental. As this unfolds, more opportunities will come your way. When you receive the gifts of others, you can show mercy to them, aided by the Holy Spirit.

The Case Study Of Sarah And The Three Visitors (Genesis 18 vs 1-15): A long time ago, God blessed Abraham and promised to make him the father of all nations. Although Abraham received this promise, it was not immediately fulfilled. It required Abraham and Sarah to have faith until something happened. One day, three men visited Abraham at the entrance of his tent. Abraham welcomed these men, bowed down to them, and asked Sarah to prepare three seahs of the finest flour and knead it to make bread. Sarah was hospitable and encouraged her family to care for these strangers. After these men finished eating, one of them said, "I will surely return to you about this time next year, and Sarah your wife will have a son" (Genesis 18:10). You can see that hospitality is a great blessing for a woman from the Lord. When you are open and help others, you may not realize the greatness they can bring to your path. Abraham had faith in and trusted God for years. Abraham and Sarah both welcomed and entertained angels without knowing this was the path to receiving the fulfillment of God's promise.

> "Abraham believed God, and it was credited to
> him as righteousness', and he was called God's friend.
> You see that a person is considered righteous
> by what they do and not by faith alone"
> (James 2: 23).

A Woman Of Hospitality

PRACTICAL APPLICATIONS
PURPOSE # 12: A WOMAN OF FAITH AND HOSPITALITY

1. How does praying transform you?
_____
_____
_____
_____

2. Discuss the results of people who prayed in their generation.

a. Paul and Silas (Act 16 vs 25) _____
_____

b. Hannah (2 Samuel 2 vs 1) _____
_____

c. Elijah (2 Kings.17 vs 19-21) _____
_____

d. Esther (Esther 4 vs 15-17; Esther 9 vs 25) _____
_____

3. What is hospitality? (I Peter 4 vs 9-11)
_____
_____
_____
_____

4. Discuss three reasons why hospitality is essential. (Genesis 18 vs 1-11)

   a. _____
   _____

   b. _____
   _____

   c. _____
   _____

5. What may be challenging to becoming hospitable?
   _____
   _____
   _____
   _____

6. Discuss possible safety measures in today's world you need to become aware of as you become hospitable.
   _____
   _____
   _____
   _____

Prayer

Lord, make me a woman of faith, a woman who is willing and obedient to fulfill your purpose and will, never doubting and always trusting in you. Grant me grace to show hospitality to others from a heart of love and compassion. Amen.

CONCLUSION

Sacrifice is the highest price a woman must pay to make a difference. These sacrifices may include your time, humility, learning new skills, self-improvement, pursuing greater knowledge, praying and fasting, leading, and taking on strategic responsibilities to advance your business, projects, leadership, home, community, and country. If you want to make a difference in this generation, rise from complacency and take tangible action. Remember, marriage or being under a man's authority is not a requirement for making an impact. God can use you based on your availability to Him and the flexibility you offer to express the Kingdom of God. Whether you are single or married, God desires you to be a vessel ready for the Master's use.

Are you prepared to make changes in your world? If you are married, have you studied your husband enough to identify his personal challenges? What strategies must you implement to embrace the flaws and imperfections in your partner or marriage? What guidance do your children need to help them serve the Lord and follow His direction? Are you coordinating your readiness with your family's to become instruments of change?

What changes are needed in your city? Does it need revival? Do you wish to see improvement and development in areas like community, resources, infrastructure, health, and finance? If you are single, are you ready to be the Mary of our generation who receives the power of the Holy Spirit to accomplish great things? If you are like the woman at the well of Samaria, will you reveal the Lord to the people around you?

If your answer is yes, what methods will you use to initiate improvement? There is no glory without a price. What is the cost of the level of influence you hope to achieve? Are you determined to reach the next level of glory and accomplishment? Do you plan to give birth to improvement? Start by putting a strategy in place, beginning with yourself. Personal revival and enlightenment will lead to family revival and can inspire others in the community.

REFERENCES

Cambridge Dictionary, s.v. "Structural," accessed October 10, 2023, https://dictionary.cambridge.org/us/dictionary/english/structural

Dairo, Rebecca. Building a Glorious Home: How to Construct a Fulfilling Marriage. Florida: Xulon Press, 2023.

Selman, Joshua. "How to Build Formidable Systems and Structures in Your Life." June 4, 2022. Educational video, 46:50. https://www.youtube.com/watch?v=SVqY_JdO0lg

All Scripture references are from the New International Version (NIV) except otherwise stated.

ABOUT THE AUTHOR

 **Dr. Olapeju Rebecca Dairo** is a life coach who focuses on strengthening family dynamics and empowering individuals. Alongside her husband, Adeniran Dairo, she runs Living Right Academy, where they teach biblical principles to help adults become effective leaders.

Rebecca supports parents—both single and married—and grandparents by providing life skills that enhance relationships, solve problems, and achieve personal goals. With over fifteen years of teaching experience in community colleges and high schools, she has successfully guided numerous students and clients toward positive change.

As a committed Christian, Rebecca's faith fuels her work while she raises her three middle-school children. Through her knowledge and practical approach, she inspires others to lead fulfilling lives based on biblical teachings.

For your Free Purpose call, visit:
https://calendly.com/livingrightacademyministry/25min

To download our special gift, visit:
https://www.livingrightacademy.com/

OTHER BOOKS BY REBECCA DAIRO

Building a Glorious Home:
How to Construct a Fulfilling Marriage

www.ingramcontent.com/pod-product-compliance
Lightning Source LLC
LaVergne TN
LVHW061625070526
838199LV00070B/6583